CW00823378

THE
Archive Photographs
SERIES

PAIGNTON

A classic photograph of Paignton's smooth red sands, which have been loved by generations of children. Arthur Hyde Dendy first provided bathing machines in the early 1870s. These were 'in ample supply for both ladies and gentlemen' and as they were drawn by horses, they were 'available at all times of the tide'.

THE
Archive Photographs
SERIES

PAIGNTON

Compiled by
John Pike and the Torquay Natural History Society

CHALFORD

First published 1997
Copyright © John Pike and the Torquay Natural History Society, 1997

The Chalford Publishing Company
St Mary's Mill, Chalford,
Stroud, Gloucestershire, GL6 8NX

ISBN 0 7524 1019 9

Typesetting and origination by
The Chalford Publishing Company
Printed in Great Britain by
Bailey Print, Dursley, Gloucestershire

Dedicated to the memory of Peter Tully.

Contents

Introduction   7

1.   Paignton: the Place   9

2.   The Harbour   23

3.   The Sea Front and Pier   27

4.   The Railway   45

5.   Buses and Trams   51

6.   Walking the Streets   61

7.   Crowds of People   69

8.   Paignton at War and the Years Between   79

9.   Sport and Pleasure - a Miscellany   83

10. At Work for Paignton   91

11. Oldway and the Singers   95

12. Goodrington, Broadsands and Churston   107

13. Stoke Gabriel   121

Acknowledgements   128

Paignton's first cycle track, complete with small grandstand, 1886. This very faded original must be one of the earliest surviving sporting photographs of Paignton. The track was situated behind the original Esplanade Hotel. The cycles used by the riders were of course penny-farthings.

Introduction

Peter Tully, to whom this book is dedicated, is worthy of having a full-length biography written about him. He had a long business career and a great involvement with Paignton Regatta; indeed, he was 'Mr Regatta' to many as he organised the firework displays for many years. It is the wish of many people in Paignton that there should be some enduring testimony to his dedication and commitment; this publication is offered to do this.

My friendship with him started relatively recently. In 1979 Peter Grafton the head of adult education at Paignton Community College pressed me into setting up a local history evening class. It was a smallish group, mostly of life-long Paigntonians but one of the most enthusiastic of my 'pupils' was Peter Tully. When the class ended, a handful remained behind discussing the pictures shown, to show their own mementoes and other 'pictures of Paignton'. This usually continued until the caretaker, keys in hand, forced us to leave the school. We then continued in the car park until he put the lights off there also. On at least one occasion the headlights of a car had to be used to take a last look at some treasure. This set Peter on his quest for pictorial material which ended only with his death soon after he retired. In a decade or so he had amassed a considerable collection which he passed to the Museum of the Torquay Natural History Society and is now known as the Peter Tully Collection. This exceptional archive, the work of one enthusiast, contains over 6,000 slides as well as hundreds of pictures and other memorabilia. Before his early decease he had used his knowledge, and his pictures, to raise money for his favourite charities. It is perhaps a measure of his love for his town and his hobby that the parish church was filled with his friends for a 'celebration of his life' rather than for a memorial service. It was a privilege to be present to hear his favourite hymns sung and listen to the tributes paid to him. He would, I am sure, have liked this book to be about Paignton, his place and his people.

Mr Ivan Martin, a member of the Regatta Committee with Peter and son of Frank Martin, a mayor of Torbay, has made his late father's large collection of nineteenth century original photographs available for this book. Many are very rare indeed and are as frail as parchment; it has however been possible to copy a proportion and, although modern photo-technology does not recapture fully their superb quality, some are able to be included here. My thanks to Ivan for his generosity.

John Pike
May 1997

Peter Tully salvaging treasures after the disastrous fire at Waycott's Corner in July 1952. He then owned Purdy's tobacconist's which was also engulfed in the flames.

One
Paignton: The Place

Paignton has had a long history as an ecclesiastical establishment. In the Middle Ages and the years after, it was used by the Bishops of Exeter as a place of rest and retirement. Much earlier, in about 700 AD Paega arrived, his home becoming known as 'the farm (tun) of Paega's people'. In the Domesday Book it was Peinton and, by the time its market and fair was granted in 1295, it was Peynton. By the nineteenth century it had become Paignton or Paington (just two of the many variations in spelling recorded). Its transition from a modest seaside village to a major holiday resort is recorded in the following prints and photographs.

The old village grouped around the church in a now-fading photograph, *c.* 1880. Much of the marshland towards the sea is still evident although building has started in what is now Torquay Road and Hyde Road. This photograph was taken before the pier was built.

A harvest scene, captured only a few years later than the previous photograph. The whole of the open ground near the Coverdale Tower has been developed. *Axworthy's Guide*, published around 1900 says that since the late 1880s 'the pier has been constructed, scores of roads opened up and hundreds of houses built, a fine Public Hall and new churches, banks and public buildings erected'. The roof of the new Public Hall is in the foreground.

This is probably the earliest surviving picture of Paignton, possibly made 200 years ago. It exists on an old paper negative, hence its poor quality. Three windmills are visible; the two in the distance can be identified as those at Galmpton Warborough (to the left of the church) and the one on Windmill Hill (to the right). Where the third (in the mid-ground) was located is less certain.

This picture is believed to be from the Frith collection. The photographer is looking down from Winner Hill on to the open land which was later developed and became Palace Avenue and Gardens. In this photograph the pier seems to be completed, so the date must be after 1879, which was when it first opened.

A photograph taken by J. Valentine from the same high ground as the previous picture but overlooking 'old Paignton'. The gasometer is prominent, so too is the old mill. Between the mill and the Torquay Road there appears to be orchards and gardens. Behind the large house in Church Street is the field called 'The Crofts' on which the Cottage Hospital was later built.

Although captioned Paignton Church, this early lithograph from the museum's C.B. Oak's Collection also shows the centre of the town perhaps 250 years ago when it had character. Note the town stocks beside the lych-gate.

The Coverdale Tower from inside the garden. Almost all the views of this important landmark have been photographed from outside.

		£	s	d
Keeping the Clock		0	5	0
Cleansing the leads & tower		0	2	6
Expended at Court		1	12	6
pd the Vicar's Dinner		0	3	0
pd for bread & wine for four Sacraments		2	6	8
pd Postage of a Letter from ye Bishop about ye Papists		0	1	0
pd Postage of a form of Prayer for ye Fast		0	1	0
pd for killing five Badggars		0	5	0
gave a poor woman & two Children with a pass		0	1	0
pd a man & Horse Carrying a man to Totness & after to justice & then to Totness again		0	2	6
To 10¾ lb. of wetted Lime & Carrage at ye four Shillings pr Ht		2	3	0
To 2½ hh. of Stone Lyme & Carrage at 3-6p		0	8	9
to boy & Horse Carring Sand		0	1	6
pd Jno Cornish for going to Totness for ye Coronor		0	1	6
pd Mossr Mosey Junr for fitching the Coroner		0	0	6
pd George finch one days work		0	1	0
pd a man & two Horses drawing a dead man from Goodrington Sands to the Churchyard		0	2	6
pd a man & two Horses drawing a dead man from Broadsands to the Churchyard		0	3	0
pd Will. Brown two days works		0	0	6
pd the Plumbers bill		15	15	0
Expended att Totness to see ye weight of the		0	4	0

A page from the Church Rate Book of 1781. The vicar's dinner cost the parish 3s 0d. The dispatch of 'five badggars' cost five shillings but the highest costs were for dealing with a body recovered from Goodrington Sands; this included 'fitching the coroner' from Totnes. The originals are in Devon Record Office.

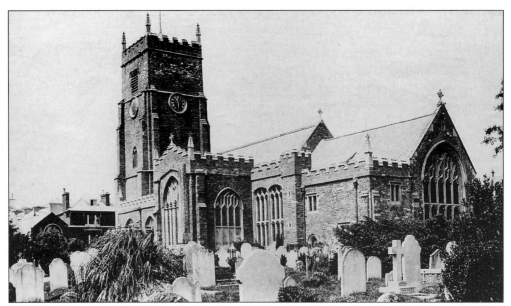

A recently discovered photograph of the parish church probably taken by J. Valentine, c. 1890. It shows how little the building had changed in 150 years. Formally known as the church of St John the Baptist, it is the third to be built on the site. The Saxons occupied Devon in the eighth century and it is possible the first Christian church was built soon after. Later it is likely a small wooden church would have replaced it. The foundations of this early edifice have been uncovered from time to time; some water-worn stones lie a few centimetres below the floor of the present church. The second church was built by the Normans in about 1100 and was a solid structure of local sandstone and imported Beer stone. Evidence of this can still be seen in the present church, which dates from about 1260. Walter Bronescombe, who was then Bishop of Exeter, initiated its building.

The interior of the church captured by the same photographer as the previous picture and probably taken at the same time.

...my a mercy to have our Rate signed — 0 — 1 — 10

Sidemen wardens Collectors meet for to
send for Sessions warrant Expended — } 0 — 3 — 2

Sent margarett Sea to Blagdon that day — 0 — 0 — 2

August 22 Receiued mary Smith from —
Stoakgabrill by and order then Expended — 0 — 9 — 0

Paidmen Collectors when they paid docteer
Penny for the Cureing of Sparks meads Legs
then Expended _____ } 0 — 1 — 6

Paid John Tully for Cloaking his Apprentise 0 — 10 — 0

more to the old Collectors for Awarrant — 0 — 1 — 0

Paid ye dockter for Cureing Sparks meads Legs 2 — 10 — 0

Paid Ann Buchel for her Apprentise Joan Neck — 1 — 12 — 0

Paid to wilmott Smith for Tending Robert Spark 0 — 3 — 0

Paid to Easter Langler for Sowing Rusel beding 0 — 0 — 6

Paid Jane Blackstone for Tending Rusel in Sicknes 0 — 4 — 0

more for Tending Rusel 1 moneth — 0 — 4 — 0

more for Tending Rusel in Sicknes — 0 — 2 — 0

for Shift for Richard Tupe — 0 — 4 — 0

Paid Symon Durbin for makeing Rows boyes Cloe 0 — 2 — 4

Paid Symon Langler for Coppiing of an order }
for Carrying Tooker to Coffenswill — 0 — 0 — 6

for boards for Rusels Bed and window Leauy 0 — 3 — 0

for wood to Philip Bartlett — 0 — 6 — 8

for Carrying Tooker 5 times to Coffenswill 0 — 4 — 0

Paid Edward Edwards for Shooes and —
mending as his bill doth Appeare — } 0 — 12 — 8

Paid John Bullard for Shooes & mending as }
his bill doth Appear — 0 — 18 — 9

Paid Clement Furneaux for Lying & wooling }
as his bill Appeareth — 2 — 8 — 6

Paid to mr Hutchings for Lyning Cloath — 0 —

Paid to Sam: Hutchings for Lyning and —
wooling Cloath as his bill Appeareth — }

A further page from the parish records showing expenditure by the Overseers of the Poor, in February 1741. The scribe had some difficulty spelling local place names such as Stoakgabrill and Coffenswill. The death of a pauper meant 'lyning and wooling', Clement Furneaux was paid £2 8s 6½d for this task. To be buried in wool was a requirement under two Acts of 1667 and 1678. It was designed to help the wool trade and the acts were finally repealed in 1814. The originals records, which date from the 1690s, are in Devon Record Office.

Looking from Primley Park towards Roundham and Goodrington. The little iron church glistening in the sunshine is St Andrews which was first used for Divine Service in 1875. It was finally replaced by the permanent building which was erected between 1893 and 1897. The building under construction nearby is the new house for Henry John Bailey (later the Marist Convent and now the Tower House School). Some of the land on the Head is still undeveloped and most of Goodrington behind the sands is arable land.

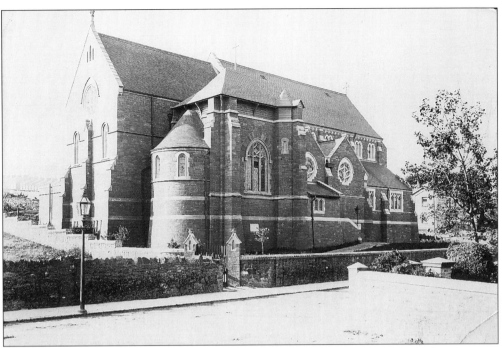

The permanent St Andrew's Church, probably photographed soon after it was built.

Christ Church, clearly a Victorian contemporary of St Andrews, taken by J. Valentine. This church was built between 1886 and 1888. The picture of the town centre featured on the next page, shows that the church was unfinished by the time of the photograph.

The Parish Church, in a location which shows how quickly the Palace Avenue area was developed in the late 1880s. It also shows how the higher ground at Polsham was already built over although much of the marsh between it and the town is still visibly unused. This picture dates from just before the Wesleyan Methodists built their new church. At the time of the photograph they were still in their old chapel at Polsham which had been built in 1868 at a cost of £600.

This photograph is inscribed with 'R.C. Church and Convent, Paignton'. In 1881 it was reported that 'a monastic order has bought a villa residence in Paignton'. The amount of the purchase money is said to be £6,000, and the house was to be used as a finishing college. It was then known as 'The Quarry'. The chapel, called the Church of Our Lady, adjoining the monastery, was built in 1882 and used as a place of worship by the Catholic townspeople. It was later said that, 'in the five years since the Marist Fathers had settled in Paignton, the number of Roman Catholics had increased from less than a dozen to about one hundred'. As numbers increased, a second church was used in Colley End Road (it was later the Mencap Centre) and the third, the present one, was erected in Cecil Road in 1932. The Marist Fathers left Paignton in the 1960s, their church, bought by the Borough Council, initially for educational purposes, was later leased to Paignton Lions Club for use as a community centre.

The growth of Preston necessitated the building of St Paul's, with the foundation stone laid by Dame Violet Wills (of the tobacco family) in January 1939. It was consecrated in the December and the first vicar was the Revd A.C. Vodden. (WMN)

The modern church of St George at Goodrington. Inside is a memorial tablet dedicated to Albert Mansbridge CH, DL, who was the founder of the Workers Educational Association and instituted the College of the Sea. He worshipped at the church.

Roundham, taken from a section of a large photograph by J. Valentine. Paignton railway station is dwarfed by the large goods shed and appears to have changed little since the late 1850s when it was first built. The stark white building is the Congregational (now United Reformed) church in Dartmouth Road. This was built in 1875-6 from local stone and has a small tower. The cost of the building was just £2,475. The land between the church and the railway line is still open fields, so too is that on the north side of the narrow way between the town proper and the Gerston.

Part of the panoramic view towards the sea. The north side of Torbay Road has been built and the Gerston Hotel is the gleaming-white building in the centre. The bridge over the railway was prominent then. In the distance the 'Wigwam', completed in the 1870s, dominates. The modest properties built all around it in the years since have had a detrimental effect on its grandeur, in spite of Paris Singer's reconstruction built early in the twentieth century. In both views the whole of the higher ground beyond is as yet not built upon.

Two

The Harbour

It is a romantic story to believe that early Paignton was built, like its neighbours, in two places. The nucleus of the village was inland, clustered around the parish church. A mile or so away was the hamlet with a small haven providing access to the sea, a vital necessity to reach the rich fish stocks in Torbay and further offshore. This separation was also crucial when invaders by sea arrived and were likely to overwhelm the people. There was time to warn the villagers of those coming to rape and pillage, thus allowing them time to hide. Much later, of course, it was the press-gang which was to be feared. Its members came ashore from ships anchored in Torbay in search of men to supplement their crews. Surviving letters show that young Paigntonians were among those who were spirited away to the hills behind as the Navy marched away from the small boats beached on Paignton Sands. Around the bay there were three distinct communities, 'Brixham Church Town' and 'Brixham Quay'; 'Tormohun' and 'Torre Quay' whilst at Paignton, the ancient quay was at 'Rowneham' (today Roundham) with the village of Peinton (it had many different spellings over the centuries) a mile inland.

91. PAIGNTON, FROM THE CLIFF.

The new harbour, captured by Mr Bedford, the well-known early photographer. The new harbour replaced the old structure which, by the 1830s, was said to be derelict. In 1837 the *Paington* Harbour Company was formed and within two years, trading schooners were landing cargoes of coal and other goods. In the background behind the harbour building is Torbay House, a large and elegant structure. As part of the development of the promenade the whole group, house and outbuildings, were razed to the ground in February 1878.

This photograph, by J. Valentine, was taken 40 years later than the previous picture. The changes around the harbour have been minimal but Torbay House has disappeared, with the pier (a little further north) taking its place. The buildings along the Esplanade are also prominent.

It was not the brightest of days when J. Valentine took this picture of the southern end of the Esplanade. It does however show that this block of buildings has changed little in the last century, indeed it might be argued that they look better in the 1990s than they did in the 1890s.

A rare photograph, by J. Valentine, of the working harbour. At this time exports included the famous Paignton cider and cauliflowers.

Paignton Harbour captured by J. Valentine. The initial cost of 'erecting two quays and harbour wall etc.' was £3, 423 10s, in 1837. Harbour records show that nearly half as much, £1, 575 10s, was allowed for 'contingences, Acts, etc.'.

The old Coastguard Station at the side of the harbour. The open door leads into the shed where the 'rocket for life-saving' was kept. At the time of the Great Storm in 1866 the cumbersome and weighty *Manby Mortar* was manhandled over Roundham to Broadsands where all the crews from the stranded ships were brought ashore safely.

The harbour, with coastal shipping, c. 1890. This remained in private hands until June 1923 when the council tried to purchase it. £2,500 was offered but this was rejected. Over a decade passed by before there were more negotiations between the council and the Harbour Company. It passed to Paignton Council under the 1936 Act. This was at the same time that the only woman harbour-master in the British Isles was appointed, Miss Stella Gale.

Three
The Sea Front and Pier

The importance of Paignton's firm red sands were appreciated even before the railway was built. A century and a half ago a glowing prospectus forecast a great future for Paignton Sands. At that time there were sand dunes between Paignton Sands and the village, and during storms the sea encroached inland. Peter's pictures show how the waves were kept at bay and how the Victorians and the Edwardians created a 'new town' between the sea wall and the railway, and beyond.

A J.Valentine photograph showing the bathing machines at the water's edge. The pier appears so pristine that it cannot yet be open to the public. Prospective bathers are waiting to purchase their tickets from the small hut near the steps. The donkeys are obviously about to start their day's work on the sands, as the tide is out.

This was probably taken by a rival photographer a few years later than the previous picture. Mr Dendy has his booking office for the Paignton Bathing Company in position and walkers are promenading on the pier. Although not busy with holidaymakers, there is an ice cream seller on the Promenade. Four shelters have also now been erected (completed in 1892 at a cost of £100 each) on the Green beyond the Sands.

Paignton Bathing Company, Ltd.

A LARGE NUMBER OF

WELL-APPOINTED BATHING MACHINES,

Fitted with every convenience, and drawn to the water's edge.

MALE AND FEMALE ATTENDANTS.

FINE, FIRM, GENTLY SLOPING SANDS.

The Safest Bathing Place in the Kingdom.

The Bathing Company eventually sold out to Paignton Council in 1921. There were then thirty bathing machines which, with the office and other equipment, cost the ratepayers £1,425. It was said that 'the modern bather does not want to be towed down to the waves so as not to be seen entering or leaving the water. They may have served some purpose in the Victorian era, today they have neither the merit of ornament nor utility'.

Towing a bathing machine down to the water's edge. The bathing season began on 1 June and terminated about 1 October.

The fair was on the south end of the Green. Apparantly, it had been there for many years but it had always been the subject of many complaints. In 1901 it was moved to the new Victoria Park but was soon moved back once again to the Green.

This photograph from the 1890s tells several stories. Mrs Penwell's lemonade stall on the Sands was the only one permitted. She paid 10s 0d (50p today) to lease the plot from the council for the season. In that year the fair was on the south part of the Green, but the following year it moved to the other end near Redcliffe. The single-horse carriage has, unusually, a postillion riding on the back step. Behind the carriage are two lady cyclists who, in the height of fashion, are sporting their bloomers. In the background is the Paignton Club, built for gentlemen only and opened in January 1885.

The southern part of the Green before any work had been carried out. The terrace is visible beyond. The exterior appearance of both the Green and the terrace have changed little in the past century.

Cottages in the old 'port of Paignton' at Roundham. They had probably been there for centuries but were demolished prior to the building of the Paignton Club just before 1882.

A panorama towards Torquay from a little further away at Roundham, in the 1880s. It was taken on one of the days that the band was playing on the roof of the Shelter. Its unique interest, however, is the landscape beyond as there are no houses at all on the hills behind Preston or at Livermead.

The newly-completed promenade visible behind the new sea wall and raised up above the level of the old marshy ground. It appears that the Paignton Club may be still under construction; the house behind, 'Kingswood', certainly is.

Both the Paignton Club and 'Kingswood' were completed at the time of this photograph. A century later and Paignton Club is little changed externally but 'Kingswood', however, is no longer there, and was demolished in the 1980s. Kingswood Court, the modern block of flats now occupies the site.

Looking south towards the Torbay Club. Whilst some wear light attire, there is still formality on the part of the gentlemen. Some older ladies wear dresses which sweep the sand as they walk.

Tents were allowed only on the north side of the pier. Initially these cost 10s 6d (a little over 50p) for the season but by about 1912 it cost visitors £2 10s (£2.50). However, residents were able to put up their own on payment of ten shillings to the council. The deckchairs are probably some of the 'seventy-five good second-hand chairs with hoods', bought in 1909.

A very different view of the tents. An unknown photographer 'snapped' the occasion. Note the date, it was not mid-winter but mid-September.

Mr J. Valentine stood in this popular spot for photographers to take this picture of holidaymakers in the late 1880s.

Paignton Sands, as remembered by many, 1959. At this time, even the then 'self-drive motor boats' were quite expensive at ten shillings (50p) a time. The Punch and Judy show was operated by Mr J. T. Stafford; some children are already sitting in place waiting for the next performance. (WMN)

Paignton crowded with holidaymakers, with the Sands and Promenade a mecca for people of all ages, August 1964. The local Rowing Club's 'four', passing from sea to shore, need to walk carefully to avoid treading on the packed sunbathers. (WMN)

The 'enclosed shelter' built in 1888. The first caretaker, a Mrs Ellis, chosen from a short list of six, worked from 8a.m. to 9.30p.m. seven days a week during the summer months for the princely sum of seven shillings (35p). Exactly why the band has scaled the ladder on to the roof is not certain. There was a small bandstand but for some reason was not being used. The large black umbrellas are being used to shield the ladies' delicate skins from the summer sun.

The shelter was, for many years, the focal part of the Promenade. It was often used for camera-stands as well as by the band. This photograph, also by J. Valentine, shows the newly-completed Torbay Road. The ornamental fountain was erected in celebration of Queen Victoria's Golden Jubilee in 1887, but was removed shortly before the building of the Festival Theatre. Note the ornamental trees on both sides of the road, the Victorians loved to line their roads with trees. However, the arrival of the motorcar soon changed the situation but the final demise of tree-lined streets in some places has been quite recent.

A Home Fleet lying in Torbay in the mid-1930s. Although well in the background, the aircraft carrier *Courageous* is anchored; she was to be one of the Royal Navy's first casualties in the Second World War.

This arch, celebrating twenty-five years of the reign of King George V and Queen Mary, was erected in 1935. It remained only for a short time as His Majesty died the following year.

This was the entrance to the promenade from Torbay Road which greeted visitors and residents after the Second World War. The flower beds were a feature of the display and, although constructed on the roadway, was complete with an ornamental pond. The windmill was removed not long before the Festival Theatre was built.

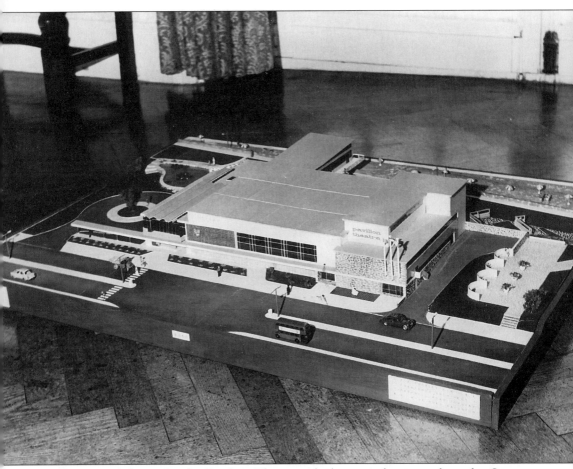

The original design for the Pavilion Theatre, which was to be situated on the Green, was exhibited at Oldway in 1965. It was designed by Thurley, a local architect. The principal change when the project became a reality was that it was called the Festival Theatre. It was given a gala opening on 10 June 1967 with a performance by the Black and White Minstrels. Throughout the seventies and eighties it remained an important venue for summer season shows, with the occasional visit from ballet companies and concerts by the Bournemouth Symphony and other orchestras.

Paignton Pier as envisaged by George Souden Bridgman, its designer. Built by the entrepreneur Arthur Hyde Dendy, it was opened in 1879.

The Esplanade Hotel as it existed in the 1880s. Bridgman's impression of the hotel captured in his sketch, matched the reality.

The brand new pier, probably before any patrons walked upon it, in the late 1880s. Behind the photographer was the Pier Pavilion which offered 'an ever-varying programme of music' whilst on Sundays 'the organ played sacred music' according to one brochure. All the hills behind Paignton are bare and without any buildings at this time.

Mr Valentine must have been an early riser to capture this view, as there was not a soul in sight, when he put up his tripod just beyond the ornamental pagodas of the pier. This was the scene nearly 120 years ago and, although there have been some changes, the properties are still recognisable.

When the Germans seemed likely to invade in 1940, a section of the pier was removed to make it less serviceable to the invading hordes. It remained like this for several years and this very poor press photograph seems to be the only one still extant.

The pier on a fine day in December 1965. Major alterations had just been completed although the final face-lift was not finished until early in 1981. The pier was sold to Mitchell Leisure (which operates the Grand Pier at Skegness) in June 1994 for a sum in excess of £0.5 million. It had been owned by the Cole Family for forty years. This photograph also shows clearly where the new construction had taken place to repair the gap shown on the previous picture. (WMN)

Four

The Railway

Isambard Kingdom Brunel had died before the railway reached Paignton but the great man continued to have a lasting influence on its construction. It was, of course, his seven foot broad gauge which brought the lines direct from London by way of Bristol and Exeter. The 'railway mania' continued, its popularity with the local gentry and others provided the finance to build it. Eventually the Dartmouth and Torbay Railway was completed from Torquay to Kingswear. The earliest of the train pictures is one of the last lithographs to be drawn on stone. The early photographers were at work in Torbay soon after 1850 and many copies of their work have survived. Some time during the 1890s the picture postcard era began. Some of the first on sale locally originated in Germany but soon the Bathes in Torquay, the Vickerys in Paignton (and others) entered the field and their postcards, produced locally, were on sale.

This engraving post-dates some early photographs. It is however of great interest because it shows the railway in about 1860 crossing open marshland between town and sea. The footbridge beside the station was to remain a familiar landmark for well over a century. Its modern successor has been sited just north of the site of the original (next door to Messrs Woolworths).

CELEBRATION OF  THE OPENING

OF THE DARTMOUTH AND TORBAY RAILWAY, TO PAINGTON, AUG. 1st, 1859;

REVIVAL OF THE ANCIENT CHARTER OF

THE WONDERFUL PAINGTON PUDDING

AND SOME PARTICULARS ABOUT IT.

THIS Pudding bore the form of a pyramid, and was gaily decorated. The ingredients were, 573 pounds of flour, 191 pounds of bread, 382 pounds of raisins, 191 pounds of currants, 382 pounds of suet, 95 pounds of sugar, 320 lemons, 144 nutmegs, and 360 quarts of milk, which made, in the aggregate, a total weight of two thousand one hundred pounds! The Pudding was made in sections, and was built up on a waggon. The procession was formed at Primley, the residence of John Belfield, esquire, at noon, from whence the cortege proceeded by way of Weston House, and through Winner-street, on by Matthews'-house, down by the Cross-road, and through Gerston-terrace to the Railway Station, and from thence to The Green, where about 3000 people of the parish of Paington, as well as the brave men who made THE LINE, all seated in a circle, partook of THE FEAST! The Pudding was a ton weight, and drawn by eight horses, there were, also, four waggon loads of beef, bread, and cider. Excursion trains ran from all parts of the county, several steamers made trips, and Mr. Anthony Nicks, the harbour-master, threw open the harbour, free. The bells sent forth merry peals. Hundreds of *pretty hats and bonnets* graced the fair forms of the daughters of Paington, and the young gentlemen of Torquay took good care to *steel* their hearts before venturing on the green! Even the old men and women who partook of a like Pudding forty-two years ago were much exhilirated by the fun. A splendid band of music attended, and beaux and belles danced on the green, while the never-ceasing waves of the beautiful and glorious sea kept time.

ORDER
OF
THE PROCESSION.
—o—
Policemen.
Navies with picks & shovels.
Waiters.
Band.
Bread, in waggon with three horses.
Committee.
Policemen. — *Waiters with Flags.* Beef, in waggon with three horses.
Beef, in waggon with three horses.
Committee.
Body of carvers.
Cider, in waggon with two horses.
Cider, in waggon with two horses.
Committee.
Waiters with Flags. — *Policemen.*

PUDDING!!
in waggon with eight horses.
Committee.
Secretary.
General
Arrangement Committee.
Policemen.
Inhabitants.

Thousands of persons visited the scene of the f tivities, and the whole must have formed a lasti feature in the memory of the youngest inhabitai A great number of those who *walked* to the fe at noon, got an attack of *night-mare* in the evenii No accident of great moment occurred, save th which happened to a certain young lady, wh er *noline* was *so large* that the carvers when getti near the bottom of the pudding actually took p session of it to keep the pudding from tumbling pieces—a wise precaution on their part, ci sidering the number of hungry boys from Torqu and Brixham who stood looking on with oj mouths. So much for the utility of *Crinoline !*

But, as it is intended to say a word or two he about the beautiful sites for building, &c., at t delightful spot, I must now pass on. Paington about three miles from the pet-spot of Dev Torquay, five from Brixham, five from Tote and eight from Dartmouth. It is situated i remarkably rich and fertile district, and the s nery around it is very beautiful, consisting wooded combes and gently rising hills, with sea and the coast of Berry Head on one hand, that approaching Portland on the other, to be si from their summits. One of the great attracti of Paington is its beautiful beach of smooth bi sand, which is nearly a mile in length. The i covered ruins of a once magnificent palace are be seen close to the church. Paington is second station of the Dartmouth and Tork Railway. May PROSPERITY long attend it a THE PEOPLE OF PAINGTON!

PRINTED ON THE GREEN, AT PAINGTON, BY JOHN ROBINSON, OF TORQUAY.—PRICE ONE PENNY.

The broadsheet on sale on Paignton Green on 1 August 1859. Contrary to its wording, this had been printed before the event - the reality was very different. Just before the pudding was scheduled to be cut up for those inside the barrier, those outside it, fearful of being deprived of a share, moved forward. Soon committee, police, pudding, guests and onlookers (perhaps some 18,000 in all) were in a seething mass on the ground, in spite of the sterling efforts of the five policemen present. When order was finally restored 'not a morsel of the delightful pudding remained'.

Passengers awaiting a train on the 'up' platform, just before the track between Torquay and Paignton was 'doubled', *c*. 1905. Although Mr Brunel's broad gauge has gone, the rails are still of the old type, laid on longitudinal sleepers with 'cross-ties'.

The 'down' platform at about the same time as the above photograph. It was a primitive affair with only a few gas lamps. Queens Park had not been built (it dates from 1901) and the privately-owned Torbay & Dartmouth Railway station now adjoins the over-bridge.

The *Torbay Express* awaits departure to Torquay, it was then virtually 'nonstop to Paddington'. This picture, from the days of British Rail, taken before the decline in the sixties and before diesels took the place of the magnificent Kings and Castles.

BR Standard No 82001 enroute from Paignton to Kingswear. Note the empty fish van at the rear; this would have been transferred to the branch train at Churston and filled with prime fish at Brixham. It was then returned to the former to be attached to a later London train. This was a daily ritual much enjoyed by passengers on the evening train.

A sight no longer seen in spite of the efforts of the Torbay & Dartmouth Railway. A Kingswear-bound train crosses the viaduct at Broadsands. A photograph taken in the days of British Rail and before 1 February 1972, when 'formal notice' was given of the closure of the Paignton to Kingswear section.

An early derailment accident at Hollacombe. The event was fully reported: 'The iron bar which connects the two points and by which they are opened and closed had been fixed at one end, the other slipped between the rails and got jammed immoveably against the woodwork. The driver, Charles Marsh and stoker William Kerswell seeing there was something wrong immediately reversed the engine and all the breaks were applied but the space was too short within which to bring up the train'. The third class carriage was next to the engine, then the second, with the first class, the most luxurious of the three, at the rear and the furthest away from the smoke and smuts.

A derailment at Goodrington seventy years later in July 1935. The engine by then was 'standard gauge' and was owned by the GWR.

Five
Buses and Trams

Around the turn of the century the first motor vehicles appeared on the streets of Paignton. Some were privately-owned but most of them were in operations providing public transport for people with a few pennies to spare for a ride to Torquay. The fare for the full distance was fourpence (about 2p) but for a shorter one only twopence (less than 1p). As a result there is a fascinating pictorial record of these early 'busses' starting with Thomas Adams' LIFU steam bus bought in 1899. He was already operating small passenger vessels from Paignton Pier and it is therefore not surprising that his first omnibus looks a little like a 'ship on wheels'.

Mr Adams' omnibus at work in Torbay Road.

The double-deck GWR bus at The Strand, Torquay. There was great rivalry between the Great Western Railway (which began running motor buses in 1903) and other local operators. Both steam and the internal combustion engine were used by the early companies, the surviving archive is quite a 'cavalcade of travel'.

On 11 July 1903 the GWR started operating between Torquay and Paignton with two motor buses, with a service provided 'every fifteen minutes when both run'. The fare for the full journey was 4d (less than 2p). There was one single and one double-decker, the Licensing Committee licensing the latter for thirty-six passengers (sixteen inside, eighteen on top and two beside the driver). By the end of the first week the company was carrying 600 passengers a day.

The GWR single-decker ready for departure. Presumably mother and child were not taken on the trip to Torquay.

The GWR proudly displays its buses and crews in Station Square, after the service to Totnes was introduced, c. 1905

An early bus, which looks more sturdy than the original which ran between the two towns, outside Paignton Station. Note that service details have been painted on by a signwriter. This practice was re-introduced in the 1990s, but did not last for very long.

The arrival of wounded soldiers at Paignton was recorded by an unknown onlooker with a 'box brownie'. The GWR and other charabanc companies provided transport to Oldway which had become a war hospital in 1914. Thousands of people saw the first convoy arrive.

A classic picture of a tram in Hyde Road at the end of its run from Torquay. The conductor has changed the 'trolley' in readiness for its return journey to the Strand. Torquay saw the arrival of trams in 1907. These were propelled along by electricity taken from beneath the road by the Dolter system. This used 'studs' in the roadway and a long 'skid' beneath the tram. These proved a failure and Paignton Council refused to have them. After its conversion to 'overhead trolleys' throughout Torquay in 1910, trams were accepted and soon they were clanging their way from Hyde Road to the town boundary at the Gas Works. The popularity of this form of transport, even after the arrival of the motor car in larger numbers, is reflected in the arrival in the town of large tramcars, with a two two-wheeled bogie, holding some seventy-six passengers. Trams ceased operating early in 1934.

TRAM SERVICE.

PAIGNTON AND TORQUAY.

Cars leave Paignton at 6.45, 7.25, 7.50, 8.7, and every 10 minutes till 9.27 a.m.; then every 5 minutes till 10.7 p.m.; then every 10 minutes till 10.37; then 10.45, 11.5

SUNDAYS : Cars leave Paignton at 12.0. 12.15, 12.30, 12.40, 12.47, and every 10 minutes till 2.47 ; then every 5 minutes till 9.54 ; then 10.5.

Cars leave Strand, Torquay at 7.5, 7.45, 8.2, and every 10 minutes till 9.32 a.m.; then every 5 minutes till 10.22 p.m.. and every 10 minutes till 10.52; then 11.5.

SUNDAYS : Cars leave Torquay at 12.15, 12.22, and every 10 minutes till 2.30 ; then every 5 minutes till 9.42 ;

An early timetable showing just how good the service was in the early days, c. 1910.

A photograph possibly taken with a small camera, showing the tight turn the tramway made from Torquay Road into Hyde Road. The wall on the right was later replaced with shops.

Tram no. 37, one of the large bogie-trams in Torquay Road. These proved popular and were well-used. Some were sold to Plymouth City Council and continued in use until the Second World War.

This is Paignton's famous steamroller at work near the Palace Hotel. This was bought in 1883 for £370 and remained in use until 1938. The town was so progressive in purchasing this 'road improver' that the council loaned it to both Torquay and Totnes for a guinea (just over £1) a day.

Lorries began to replace horse-wagons for deliveries soon after the First World War. These Starkey, Knight and Ford lorries were probably in use in the early 1920s. Note the solid tyres (although pneumatics were fitted at about this time) and the beautifully polished brass headlamps which were lighted by acetylene gas. In the early days the requirement to show lights after dark were enforced by local bye-laws and 'such lamp (or lamps) to be properly trimmed, lighted and attached'.

The Salvation Army await departure on a day's outing in 1911. These 'horse-brakes' were a popular means of transport for many years up to the arrival of the charabanc. Note the steel 'skid' hanging in front of the rear wheel, this was the brake on steep hills.

Local businesses enjoyed outings in the days of the horse, but with the arrival of the new motor charbancs outings continued and were enjoyed by even larger numbers of employees. Messrs Evans' bakery await departure from New Street. Note the 'hard tyres' and the brass-work on the Daimler, including the acetylene lamps, have been newly polished.

Mr S. Batten's annual outing ready to leave from near Winner Street probably in the late 1920s. At least two of these are Lancias, a popular choice by a number of operators after the First World War.

The 1906 Rolls Royce on the Green for the carnival in 1950. In the background is the 'Tent', officially known as 'The Bandstand', although its name was changed to the 'Summer Pavilion' in 1953. Note that the top was open and the audience would have been subjected to the effects of wind and rain.

Two newspaper photographs from the 1950s and 1960s which have become of value thirty years after they were taken. Over the years Paignton has hosted displays of historic vehicles, these are from just two of them. (Both WMN)

Six
Walking the Streets

There is little evidence today of the appearance of Paignton in 'olden days'. The shopping centre is on both sides of the railway although the largest part is inland near the church. At the corner of Kirkham Street is one of Paignton's most elegant buildings, Kirkham House, also known as Priest's House.

Kirkham House is a crown property in the care of English Heritage. It probably dates from the fourteenth or early-fifteenth century and is certainly earlier than the Tudor period. It might have been provided for one of the more important officials at the palace or was the home of a priest of the Kirkham Chantry. Alternatively it could have been the residence of an important tradesman. Work of the highest standard was carried out on Kirkham House after its gift to the nation in 1960. It has a timbered doorway, a cobbled passage flanked by timber screens and a hall which reaches to the roof at one point. The rooms contain appropriate but not contemporary furniture. (WMN)

The story of Paignton as it was a century ago. The photographer was standing in Station Square looking towards Victoria Street (completed some years earlier) when he took this picture. The retail premises of the Plymouth and Torquay Breweries offers 'wholesale and retail cask and bottled ale'. Palk & Sons display fine carcases of lamb outside on hooks but no public health inspector would allow this today.

Palace Avenue in the 1890s. The trees lining the road are a fairly recent addition and still have their wooden-stake supports. The 'pianos for hire' sign is outside Charles Heaviside's music shop. It was in the flat above that his brother Oliver developed a form of mathematical calculus. Discoverer also of the 'Heaviside Layer' in the ionosphere (so important to radio communications), he was later described as ' a man of towering genius who ranks among the highest this country has produced'.

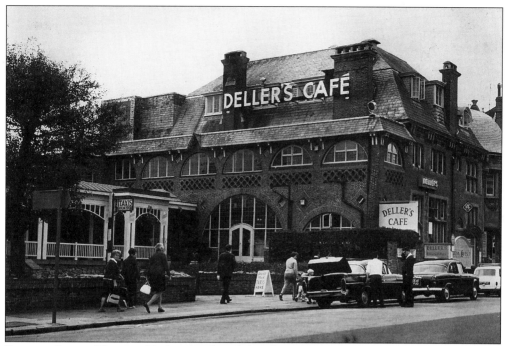

Paignton Picture House in Torbay Road made headlines recently as one of the earliest purpose-built cinemas in Europe, but even more loved was Deller's Cafe nearby. Its demise is still recalled with regret thirty years after its demolition. When this closed in 1965, part of 'elegant old Paignton' was lost for ever. (WMN)

This view of the ground floor cafe at Dellers is quite stiff and formal. Many older people will recall with affection social events they attended there.

Starkey, Knight and Ford's brewery which remained part of the Paignton scene until comparatively recent times. An ability to brew ale meant that it was able to survive competition from outside. It has now been replaced by St John's Court, an elegant replacement but its inclusion is not justified here.

Palace Avenue soon after it had been laid out taken by J. Valentine. Deller's Supply Stores site is now occupied by Rossiters. The first attempt to light the town by electricity was made in 1882 but nothing came of it as, at that time, the electric light was considered only as an alternative to gas and oil. In October 1896, Dellers became the first store to use electrical lighting, probably nearly a decade after this picture was taken.

A later view looking into Palace Avenue, the trees have now grown thicker and the top of the Public Hall can just be seen peeping through the branches. It was even more peaceful than it appears, the horseless carriage in the foreground was stuck on with glue. This would not, of course, have been visible on the postcards which were made from this 'original'.

The people on this photograph were present when the camera lens clicked. Note that the lady with the pram was moving too fast for its movement to be halted. The occasion was possibly the coronation of King Edward VII, hence the crown above the entrance to the street.

The upper storeys have not changed a great deal but Maypole Corner (or more correctly Victoria Square) has long gone. Earlier, there had been the imposing Naval Bank but in this twenties or thirties photograph, its premises are long gone. The opposite corner is now filled by the Tesco supermarket.

Torbay Motor & Engineering Company was in Torquay Road when this photograph was taken just after 1900. It should be noted that even then there was competition from the continent; the company sold Mercedes and Renaults. It also offered cars for hire even then. Torbay Motors continue in business today.

H. G. PERKINS,

GENERAL
ELECTRICAL AND MOTOR
- ENGINEERING WORKS. -

 ### OFFICIAL REPAIRER TO
- - M.U. AND A.A. - -

GARAGE FOR 30 CARS.
LARGEST GARAGE IN THE TOWN.
Sole District Agent for Swift Cars.
Any Make of Car Supplied.
CARS FOR HIRE.
Agent for Singer and B.S.A. Cars.
Tyres, Petrol, Oils, Accessories. etc., always in stock.

Totnes and Dartmouth Roads.

Mr Perkins owned a rival garage and this was in Totnes Road. Now gone, the road joining the Dartmouth and Totnes Roads passes across the site. At this time BSA Cars were still being made, plus Swift which was also a British manufacturer.

Dey's Stores in Church Street. Slogans have changed little over the years. Passers-by were being urged to 'buy now and save money'.

Frank Martin's when his premises were in Winner Street. The bicycle is of interest, it has a dynamo to power front and rear lights.

Seven
Crowds of People

There is almost a limitless supply of 'people pictures' in the Tully archive. However, even the comedians look serious. Many of the originals came from his friends and only they could 'name names'. In most cases, however, the source is unknown.

A turn-of-the-century picture of crowds on the Promenade. This is many years before the the first bandstand was erected on the Green, which did not take place until 1920. The vessel moored at the pier-end appears to be the *Prince Edward* (later of course the *King Edward*). She was launched in 1901 and called at Paignton daily.

This 'triumphal' arch of vegetation was built in Conway Road to celebrate the coronation of King George V and Queen Mary in June 1911.

The K-nuts assemble for a group photograph in May 1919. Paignton was on the verge of enjoying its first summer season after the First World War so the newspapers were full of the professional shows just 'opening for business'. This group failed to get even a brief mention.

This formidable group of ladies are from St Andrew's Girls Club in April 1922. Among those identified is Mrs Taylor, the minister's wife, standing at the back on the right.

The assembled cast of *Hit the Deck* early in 1936. In spite of its efforts the Paignton Operatic Society made a loss of £17 13s on the production. The honorary treasurer explained the reasons for this saying that 'performance rights had increased by 18 guineas, and, hire of the band parts was eight guineas'. In the late 1990s each production costs many thousands of pounds to stage.

Paignton Parish Church bell-ringers on duty possibly in the late 1940s. The four on the right were: Charlie Austin, Bill Allwood, Alf Pope and George Langworthy.

Charles Shadwell and His Orchestra, Paignton, 1954

Charles Shadwell and his orchestra during their summer season at Paignton in 1954. Summer Pavilion was not used until the 1953 season so it was under this name that the orchestra played 'with charming sweet singer Elizabeth James'. The BBC pianist Ken Phillips also had a special billing. There were many feature nights including: Tuesday, talent night, Wednesday, party night, Friday, community singing and Saturday, top tunes and dance competitions. Reserved seats cost 3s, 2s 6d and 2s. Unreserved were just one shilling (5p today). The Summer Pavilion was demolished (with the adjacent shelter, conveniences and ornamental gardens) to make room for the Festival Theatre which opened in June 1967.

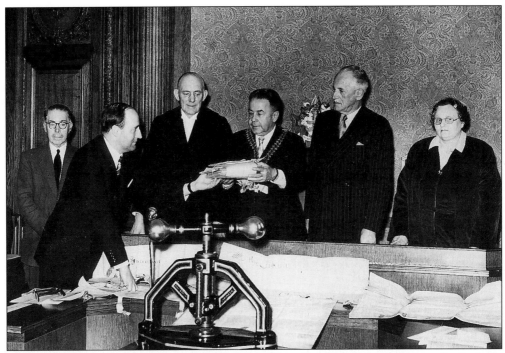

An important day for Paignton, when the old Urban District Council became 'lord of the manor' in 1959. Captain A.J. Tremeer was then chairman and the lordship was handed over on behalf of the Templer family, who had held it since 1794. (WMN)

Folk dancing on the lawn by local schoolchildren at Oldway in June 1964. Over thirty years later, it would be interesting to find out how many of the dancers still reside in the town. (WMN)

The Torquay and Paignton Gas Company shows its latest labour-saving house wares to a full house at the Public Hall in April 1937. The audience seems happy to be seated in chairs more suited to Paignton Sands. An Ascot water heater was on offer for sale at a penny-a-day. Cookers have changed little in size, but the refrigerator would have filled a small kitchen.

Prior to the arrival of the National Health Service, Paignton Hospital relied on some income from the proceeds of the carnival. The popularity of the event can be gauged from the number of people waiting for the procession, this was sometime in the 1920s when it was obviously very well attended.

A similar view to the previous photograph, but on this occasion the people are thronging the sea front. Just visible in the background are the bathing machines, no longer drawn down to the sea but 'in line' to provide a bathing station.

This photograph was found uncaptioned and undated. It is clearly a float at one of the carnivals and could be from any year from the late 1920s onward.

This is the Cottage Hospital which relied so much on the support of the carnival. Although one had been established in 1878, the one shown here was set up under a deed signed by Washington Singer (as founder), his brother Mortimer and seven others. This granted a field called 'The Crofts', with a frontage of 243 feet, in which a hospital and dispensary would be built. One proviso in the deed was that 'no one (to be) admitted suffering from an infectious or incurable disease, or is not at the time living within the parishes of Paignton and Marldon'. The people of the town were thus safeguarded.

The Countess Mountbatten, as Superintendent-in-Chief, visits Paignton to inspect the local branch of the Red Cross and St John in 1957. She died three years later whilst on a tour of the Far East. (WMN)

This familiar picture usually appears as a holiday snap. Clearly the men from the brewery are dressed up for a day's outing. It is however, a part of old Paignton now lost for ever as ales and stouts are no longer brewed in smaller breweries.

Eight

Paignton at War and the Years Between

The waters of Torbay have been filled with ships of war for several centuries but only rarely have the people of Paignton become involved. One such occasion was the grounding of HMS Venerable at Roundham early in the nineteenth century when the townspeople disgraced themselves by pillaging the wreck. Many men joined up in both wars and died for their country. During the First World War Oldway became a war hospital and many young battle-scared men recuperated there. In 1943 the Americans arrived and practised 'wet landings from the sea' with their DUKWs in preparation for D-Day. The Royal Air Force set up Initial Training Wings in Torbay, one was located at Oldway and many air-crew started to learn to fly there. Nearly 50,000 cadets in all passed through the five Initial Training Wings.

Station Square at a time of celebration. This is believed to be shortly after the relief of Mafeking during the war in South Africa. This was a great day and in the schools, after the singing of the national anthem, the children were given the rest of the day off.

The *Daily Mail* plane on Paignton Green in 1914. It was an Avro 504 and, except that this was a land plane with undercarriage, its general design is little different from the post-war seaplanes used by Captain Truelove on Preston Sands.

New recruits for General French's Contemptible Little Army march down Winner Street after a recruitment day in Paignton. New Street is in the background and T.M. Perrett's shirts can clearly be seen on display in the shop window beyond.

Captain Truelove, formerly of the Royal Air Force, offered flights in his Avro seaplane from Preston Beach, commencing in May 1919. The flight cost £1 5s. (£1.50 today), quite expensive for the time. Safety was guaranteed as 'seven compartments in the floats made the plane virtually unsinkable'. There are still people alive who remember their adventures and 'skimming just a few feet above the water'.

Unveiling the memorial to those men of Paignton who gave their lives in the war, which was dedicated in June 1921. It was said that Paignton 'with a population of 13,000 had sent 2,000 men to the war and 350 made the supreme sacrifice'. It was also reported that 'the task of the committee has not been a light one. The financial stress which followed in the wake of war has made the raising of funds a trying work. There had been labour disputes at the quarries; as a result the funds originally raised have failed to cover the liabilities of the committee and in due course another effort will be made to wipe off the deficit'.

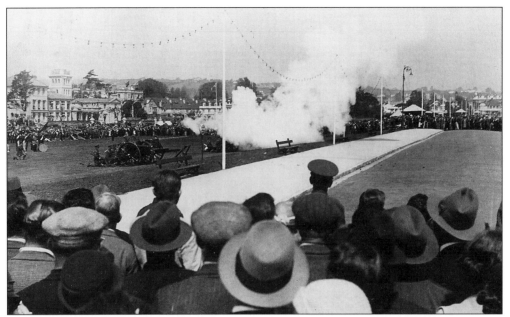

The local Royal Artillery Territorials fire a royal salute on Paignton Green in May 1935. This was part of the celebrations to commemorate the silver jubilee of the reign of King George V and Queen Mary.

Possibly a Remembrance Day parade. This could be during the Second World War or just after, as the air raid shelter is still in Palace Avenue (although the entrance is boarded up). The letters EWS tell us that there was an 'emergency water supply' nearby and older people remember them as 'static water tanks'. Some of those on parade were veterans of the First World War.

Nine
Sport and Pleasure - a Miscellany

Provision for sports men and women was first catered for in the present century. The land for Queen's Park was purchased in 1898. Filling it in started in 1900 when '3,000 tons of earth was bought for tenpence a load delivered'. After the official opening in 1901 it was used for a variety of events. Attempts to build a skating rink there were unsuccessful but bowls players had more success, a bowling green and pavillion was completed in 1937.

Among the first users of Queen's Park was the Archery Club. Paignton Rugby and Hockey Clubs were first given sole use of it as long ago as 1908.

Unfortunately this souvenir photograph of the Paignton Hockey Club team is undated and uncaptioned, but it must contain men who contributed to the town in other ways in later years.

Regatta time, 1907. These young men won the Junior Championship of the West of England the previous year in August 1906.

Fred Spencer's Comic Cricket XI played Paignton Cricket Club on 10 August 1910. There must be many players who wish they could go to the crease protected by a bat of these proportions.

The 'writing on the ball' helps identify this fine body of young men. It reads: Primley AFC, 1925-26.

The YMCA was started in Victorian times but a major change came in May 1969 when the new Youth Centre was opened at Clennon Valley, away from the town centre. The castle at Torquay was sold at about the same time. The organisation were honoured by the attendance of the Queen Mother. Although this photograph was taken nearly thirty years ago, it shows what a young sexagenarian she was.

Victoria Park soon after it was completed. Attempts to acquire the marshy ground between the Hyde Road willow plot and Victoria Road were first made in 1891. The Dendy Trustees refused to sell so it was bought by compulsory purchase in 1894 for £1,976. Its layout began a year later. When its pond was completed at the end of 1895, the council was given a swan, possibly the one in the photograph. One of the councillors promised to look after it during the winter. Although the Regatta Fair had been on the Green for many years, in 1901 the council allowed Hancock's to 'stand' in the new park. This did not continue for long as there were massive protests from the public.

Victoria Park.

In the early days, the zoo's entrance was a modest one. The entrance in Totnes Road is still almost traffic-free at the time of this photograph.

The animals on display have attracted many photographers over the years. These pumas were visited by the crew of *HMS Puma* at anchor in Torbay in 1965. The crew, expecting to see their ship's mascots, had their hopes dashed when both decided to sulk in the back of their cage and refused all attempts to be coaxed into the public gaze. (WMN)

Paignton has one claim to fame in theatrical circles. The world premiere of the *Pirates of Penzance* took place there in 1879. It was performed at the Royal Bijou Theatre built in 1870. This rather forbidding picture shows it soon after and, of course, before the fields (where Victoria Street now stands) were built over. It also shows the bus to Torquay which ran three times in each direction daily, the last departure was after the evening performance had ended. The theatre was a Victorian extravaganza, described as 'a miniature affair not much larger than a good-sized drawing room'. It was said to be tastefully fitted, the walls covered with oil paintings in gilt frames, paintings which were commissioned 'of a higher standard than usually encountered'.

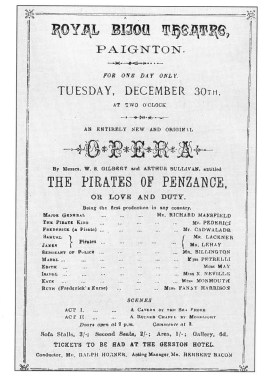

The D'Oyley Carte Company came from the theatre at Torquay and played in their 'Pinafore' costumes, wearing handkerchiefs in place of their sailors' caps. This was done for copyright reasons as shorthand takers attended first performances of the vastly-popular G & S works and pirate copies were on sale on the streets within days.

Mr Dendy's Gerston Hotel viewed from the front. This picture is quite early, before the development of Station Square. In the centre is the wooden footbridge over the railway which appeared in an 1860s lithograph.

The footbridge is still little changed in this photograph taken sometime in the 1950s or 1960s. The gates were replaced with barriers in November 1976. A Judy Holliday and Kirk Douglas picture is showing at the Odeon at Preston. It had ceased to be the Palladium by this time. The footbridge was later rebuilt to enable the road over the level-crossing to be widened.

Ten
At Work for Paignton

Nearly a century and a half ago there were worries about walking at night in the dark streets. A 'Committee for Public Lights' was formed and it first resolved that public lights should only be ignited in winter. However, a strange decision was made in 1872 that 'public lamps are not lighted after the moon is eight days old until the second day after it is full and that the lamps are put out one hour after the moon rises, provided they are always put out at 12 o'clock p.m.'. In 1876 all was changed and the surveyor was authorised to order 'the lighting of the public lamps on dark nights whatever the age of the moon'.

In 1859 a committee of prospective gas company shareholders expressed the desire to be in control of their own affairs and not to be linked with the existing Torquay and St Marychurch companies. As a result, the Paignton Gaslight, Coal and Coke Company was formed in 1859 and works were built between Mill Lane and Churchward Road. In 1923 the inevitable happened and the two companies became one. Torquay had built its works at Hollacombe (or Hollicombe) in the early 1860s and, although this photograph is dated 1936 (after it became the Torquay and Paignton Gas Company), the changes made since that time had been minimal. Production ceased in 1968 and the plant demolished soon after in February 1969. North Sea Gas arrived in Torbay in 1973. The whole site has now been converted into a pleasure ground with access to the beach below.

Torbay suffered badly from 'tip-and-run' raiders during the Second World War. Attacks on vital services like the gas works were feared and so defences were put up on the sea side of the works. As well as a rocket-battery, a Lewis-gun was kept at the ready.

The Gas Works at peak production soon after the war, c. 1947. Coal was probably still arriving from South Wales and Yorkshire, although it was also landed at Kingswear and taken the short journey from there by rail. Late in the nineteenth century electric lighting began to replace the gas. Initially the council sought to build a generating station in Queens Park and, soon after, at the harbour. Both ideas came to nothing and eventually it was a private company which provided the supply from a back-street location. However, this was not until 1908 and there were just eight customers at first. In the 1920s the town began to receive current from Torquay and the little independent operation closed down.

This formal study shows members of the Paignton Fire Brigade with all the other people associated with it. This Shand-Mason engine was bought in 1907 and was its showpiece for some years and occasionally even attended fires in Torquay. In 1910 a new fire escape was bought for £65 10s and a year after that Mr J.S. Huggins took charge. He was to have a long association with the town, later becoming a councillor.

Paignton's first motor fire engine which was bought in 1920. Note the solid tyres, these were not replaced with pneumatics until 1930. The town's second engine, bought in 1938, was also a Leyland.

A more formal photograph of the new fire engine. The first fire cover was provided by the West of England Fire Office (an insurance company) but in 1889 the company gave its engine to the Local Board. This was an elderly manual engine but it remained the only proper piece of fire-fighting equipment until 1907. It was kept in Palace Avenue secured with a padlock and chain.

During the Second World War, women were required to take the place of some of the men. The NFS insignia is just visible. Paignton Fire Brigade had ceased to exist in August 1941 when the National Fire Service came into being. Devon Fire Brigade took its place in April 1948.

Eleven
Oldway and the Singers

Isaac Merritt Singer, the inventor of the sewing machine which bears his name, arrived in South Devon from France and sought an estate to purchase. He settled on 'Fernham' at Preston and with George Souden Bridgman as architect, began building the 'Wigwam'. Sadly, he died in 1873 before his 'dream house' was finished. Externally, Oldway has changed little since Paris Singer's rebuilding although much now serves as offices for the borough council. It also has the Marriage Room for civil marriages, certainly one of the most elegant venues anywhere.

Isaac Merritt Singer, the founding father, is pictured here in a formal portrait wearing his favourite dressing-gown, 1870. The photograph was found, quite by chance, in the basement at Oldway, but it is unlikely that it had been there from his time.

The 'Wigwam' as envisaged by its architect George Souden Bridgman. Isaac Merritt was obsessed with stage life, he played minor parts in plays during tours in the USA. When he built his dream house, it was complete with small theatre with stage and auditorium (see small inset plan).

The reality: the completed Wigman design. This shows the east and south fronts and gives an indication of its large size. Clearly a mansion of this magnitude would dominate the skyline of Victorian Paignton

STABLING & EXERCISING PAVILION, PAIGNTON, TORQUAY.
GEO. SOUDON BRIDGMAN, ARCHITECT.

The Riding Pavilion as envisaged by Bridgman and, in fact, built before the house. This has survived for well over a century, having been, at various times, a film studio, factory and offices. Now (1997) it is possible it will become a theatre, offering theatre-in-the-round, among other activities.

The Riding Pavilion and, more importantly, the vast conservatory which was erected between it and the 'Wigwam'. A now-faded photograph which clearly shows the view from the rear. The car park now occupies much of the area where the glass structure stood.

The remainder of the north side viewed from a different angle. The portion to the left of the picture remains little changed from its appearance in the 1870s.

LOT 1.

(Edged Green on Plan.)

THE VALUABLE

FREEHOLD AND COPYHOLD ESTATE,

LYING ENTIRELY WITHIN A RING FENCE,

BOUNDED ON THREE SIDES BY THE

OLDWAY ROAD & TORQUAY ROAD,

To each of which it has most Commanding and Important Frontages, for the main part enclosed by a Costly Rough-hewn Stone Wall surmounted by Ornamental Iron Palisading, with massive and costly Iron Folding Gates and a Serpentine Drive of easy access, bordered by a thriving Plantation of Shrubs conducts to

THE MANSION

Built in the Italian Style of Architecture, in a most substantial manner, of Brick with Stone Dressings, having a Southern Aspect, and commanding a fine Sea View, while to the West lies the picturesque and rising Town of Paignton with a charming prospect to the Hills beyond.

It is called "The Wigwam."

And is entered under, and through a

MAGNIFICENT WINTER GARDEN.

Stone Steps lead to a pair of massive Folding Doors which open into the VESTIBULE, the Floor of which is laid in Encaustic Tiles and the Walls relieved by Panelled Dado,

AN ARCHWAY SEPARATES THE

MAIN HALL, GRAND IN ITS PROPORTIONS AND ELEGANT IN ITS DECORATIONS,

The Floors richly tiled, the colour and design being effective in their harmony, the Ceiling panelled in gold.

A page from the sale catalogue which shows for the first time what a magnificent mansion Isaac Merritt had created in Paignton.

Is Lavatory and w.c., and an elegantly-decorated MORNING ROOM. On the right is Cloak Room and Door leading to STEWARD'S APARTMENTS, and minor Staircase.

Facing the Grand Staircase is a CORRIDOR OF FINE PROPORTIONS decorated to correspond with the Hall, at the end of which are French Casements opening to a Terrace. Out of this Corridor on the left is the PROPERTY ROOM appertaining to the Theatre, SMOKING ROOM, and

SPACIOUS AND LOFTY BILLIARD ROOM

With Casements to Terrace, the South Casement opening under a Portico, Aberdeen Granite Columns supporting the Balcony above. On the right is

THE THEATRE STAGE AND AUDITORIUM,

AND BEYOND ARE

TWO NOBLE BALL ROOMS,

The Floors laid in Parquet, and communicating by Sliding Doors, the Ceilings painted in Medallions, Scrolls, and Emblematic Designs.

SLIDING DOORS AGAIN OPEN TO A

FINE SUITE OF RECEPTION SALOONS,

The Walls and Ceilings panelled in richly-toned tints, and gilded in elegant taste.

These Saloons comprise ANTE DRAWING ROOM, entered from the Grand Hall, and TWO OTHER DRAWING ROOMS, with Sliding Panels and Bays, each fitted with White Marble Mantelpiece, and having French Casements opening to the Terrace; handsome DINING ROOM, with access and communication to Drawing Room and Ante-Drawing Room, with Service Door to the Kitchen; BATH ROOM, Lavatory, w.c.; BREAKFAST ROOM, and SUITE OF BACHELORS' APARTMENTS in Four Rooms.

At the head of the principal Staircase is a

Large Square Landing with Lantern Light,

And TWO CORRIDORS, the one terminating in an entrance to the Gallery round the Winter Garden, and the other with French Casements on to the Balcony.

There are in the South Front PRINCIPAL BED ROOM and DRESSING ROOM, with Lobby and Warbrobe Closet,

A page from the sale catalogue.

100

The east front of the Wigwam under scaffolding. Between 1904 and 1907 it was rebuilt by Paris Singer in the style of the Palace of Versailles. It is said that his Italian workmen upset the people of the town as they worked on the Sabbath and at church-going time.

A magnificent study of the modern Oldway in the Spring of 1964. In the light of the morning sun, it shows off well the colonnades and the formal garden in the grounds, which were laid out by French landscape artist Duchesne. This Italian garden has fine traditional patterns with dwarf box hedging. The remainder of the grounds, steps and walls, are in keeping with the style of the building. (WMN)

This black and white photograph cannot do full justice to the magnificent ceiling which Paris included in his new building. This is a Lebrun design and permission was given for scaffolding to be erected in the Galerie des Glaces at Versailles, where there was a similar ceiling, so that the artist could achieve the correct colours. Restoration work has been carried out recently. (WMN)

This gives a clear view of the elaborate ornamentation at the top of the staircase. The gallery is also modelled on the Gallery of Mirrors at Versailles and the floor is parquet in its design. A small part of one of the huge mirrors can be seen in the background. (WMN)

Another fine picture of the staircase with the representation of the Roman god of war. This staircase of Italian marble was also built to the plans of the French architect Lebrun (who also designed one for Versailles but which was never erected). The void between staircase and ballroom is now filled with the magnificent copy of the David painting (now in the Louvre) of the *Crowning of Napoleon in Notre Dame by the Pope*. It has been made possible for the 25 x 15 feet canvas to be recreated by using computer methods from a colour transparency. (WMN)

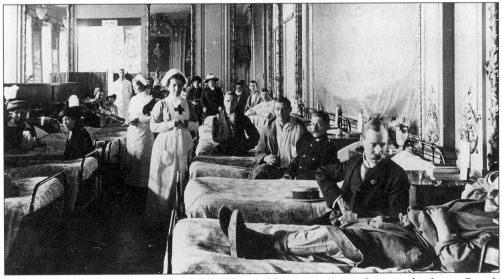

A completely different use for the ballroom. This quite rare photograph shows British servicemen recuperating at the American Women's War Relief Fund hospital which Paris Singer had made available. Initially there were 150 beds but at the time of the Battle of the Somme there were 250. By 1918, after the USA entered the war, wounded Americans were sent there to recover. However, over 100 were to die from influenza. They were buried in Paignton cemetery, the bodies being exhumed later and taken to the States.

Another ward full of wounded soldiers. A scrapbook kept by one visitor confirms that most patients came from the Western Front but some also from the disastrous Dardanelles adventure. The latter came straight from the hospital ships to Oldway. Wounded New Zealanders also occupied beds there.

(NOT TRANSFERABLE.)

AMERICAN WOMEN'S WAR HOSPITAL,

OLDWAY HOUSE, PAIGNTON.

Permit _Miss Outfin & Miss Langdon_

To Visit _Sapp. Wright_

Ward _Surg_

on the _31_ day of _Dec_ 1915

A visitors' card issued to Miss Outfin and Miss Langdon permitting them to visit Sapper Wright in 1915.

This is a 'dig for Victory' picture from the Oldway Hospital. Presumably the nurses volunteering to work in the garden were off-duty. This land was later made into tennis courts.

This little chapel was built in the Oldway grounds. Peter Tully comments that possibly more funerals were conducted here for those who died from influenza than had died from wounds.

The Redcliffe is usually associated with Colonel Robert Smith who built the eccentric building in 1856. Paris Singer bought it in 1893 (he allowed it to be used as a hospital for wounded soldiers during the South African War) and began developing the land around soon after.

As part of his plans, Paris proposed to build houses along Preston Green, envisaging seven houses in the grounds of the present hotel and fourteen houses with large gardens (excellent marine residences he called them) on the seaward side of a new drive he intended building. He completed his 'marine drive' but instead of building on the seaward side, he offered the six acres to the council for an open space (at a cost of £6,000). The transaction was completed in 1913 but nothing more could be done until the twenties. It was used for military training and trench digging in the First World War. The railway station in the background was Preston Platform, but it was only in use for about two years.

Twelve

Goodrington, Broadsands and Churston

Goodrington has appeared in documents for centuries and the scribes adopted a number of spellings, including Gorrenton Sands in the seventeenth century. During the French wars in the very early nineteenth century, Dr Thomas Trotter, physician to the Navy, set up a naval hospital in a 'large dwelling house near the beach'. This prevented the existing situation at Dartmouth where the sick sailors 'lay in sick quarters two and two in a bed'. There was a graveyard, which has now washed away, adjacent to the hospital and only one memorial stone survives. Until relatively recent times it was admired for its firm sands and safe bathing. The Great Western Railway opened a small station there in 1928, which proved popular and became the destination for day-trippers from all over Devon. After the closing of the railway from Paignton to Kingswear in 1974, the decision of the steam-hauled Dartmouth and Torbay Railway to keep the halt open, brought a new generation of 'buffs' to ride on, and photograph, the trains arriving and departing from its platforms. More recently, the construction of the Quaywest water park brought other enthusiasts by road as well. The development of the 'Brewers' Fayre' at the old hospital is now also completed.

A tranquil scene on the North Sands at Goodrington about a century ago, and of course before there was any commercial development.

A slightly later view of North Sands, note that development has already started. The first tea-stall appeared on the North Sands in 1919, the successful concessionary paying just five shillings (25p) for the season. The general beauties of Roundham Head were however to remain until the late 1920s when the Cliff Gardens and Promenade, a major construction took place. These were opened by the Hon A.V. Alexander in September 1931.

The official party planting a commemorative tree. Many of the original trees and shrubs were given by Herbert Whitley of Primley. Except for the wealth of plants now on the slopes, the scene has changed little in the sixty years since.

An early-Autumn scene in 1964. This development had started with the purchase of Goodrington Cottage from the Misses Brown in 1922, it had however to await demolition until 1935. This part of the park was completed in 1936 at a cost of £54,000 when it was opened by Sir Robert Horne. (WMN)

The Scootaboats on the lake behind in North Sands. The renewal of this small-size fleet was one of the first tasks undertaken after the Second World War, fifteen were replaced in 1946.

Motor launches first began to ply between Paignton and the Retreat in 1909, one can be seen approaching the landing-stage. The small beach tents were supplied on a commercial basis by Mr Langford. He had provided deckchairs on the Paignton Sands until the council bought its own in 1909. These were described as 'seventy-five good second-hand chairs with hoods and sundry others'.

Almost the same spot only a few years later. There is no indication that the 'larger improved version' of the tents meant that Mr Langford was still the owner. Certainly between 1920 and 1924, when acquiring land there, the council was providing its own tents.

The purchases of land had been put to good use by the 1960s. Many now grown-ups will remember those trampolines behind the beach which could be used and enjoyed for a few coppers a time.

Council workmen prepare Grange Court Holiday Centre for the summer season in 1960. Note the proud boast that it was under the control of Paignton UDC (as it then was). The town had holiday camps from the 1920s. Indeed they were so extensive in the late 1930s that one, Warners, was used as an internment camp for 'enemies of Britain' (some of the inmates had only just escaped from Nazi Germany). It was later to become a base for the US army, its troops were in the south-west waiting for D-Day. (WMN)

Waterside Camp sometime in the 1950s. This camp also became municipally-owned. Under private ownership until 1939, when it was sold to the council for £17,000, it was described as the 'only municipal camp in Britain'. This day was an important one for Torbay, the Royal Yacht *Britannia* is at anchor between the camp and Brixham.

This nineteenth-century view was taken from the high ground not far from the main Paignton to Brixham road before any building development had taken place. The viaduct is of course the first of the two built by the old Torbay & Dartmouth Railway which opened as far as Brixham Road (later Churston Station) in 1861. This, with its neighbour, is now 'scheduled'.

A mid-twentieth century photograph of a similar view to the previous picture. The need to improve communications between Paignton and Brixham involved making a cutting through Goodrington Quarry hill. This was done in 1968 but the stone removed was not discarded; it was transported to the latter port and used in the new fish wharf which was then under construction. (WMN)

An engraving from the *Illustrated London News* showing dramatically some of the vessels wrecked in a great storm at Broadsands in January 1866. The accompanying report reads that so rough was the sea it was not until 'Captain Jeffrey Searle and his two sons, finding that ropes could not be thrown to them, volunteered to swim to the ships in cork jackets. These offers were accepted and they succeeded in taking the ropes to the ships, amid enthusiastic cheers of the assembled crowd. By this means the crews were safely brought ashore'. In this Torbay storm some fifty ships were wrecked and more than one hundred lives lost.

This undated happy group was taken in happier times on Broadsands Beach. On the back of the photograph is written: Frank and Ted (with) Bobbie Wilson.

A crowded Broadsands probably in the late 1950s or early 1960s. It shows just how popular Torbay's beaches can be. The modernistic cafe replaced the hut in the early seventies.

In 1958 an important neolithic find was made by a Mr Bellville at Broadsands. Described as 'a chambered tomb', it was excavated with great care by some of the best-known westcountry archaeologists of the day. Bones found included those of an early male 'not less than 5 feet 6 inches tall and a young male less than twenty'.

This shows the excavation work at an early stage. The large stone on the right of the picture is the capstone.(WMN)

The find was in a field called Shilstone and this shows its location on the sea side of the Broadsands viaduct which is clearly visible in the background. (WMN)

Mr E.T. Vachell was the director and is seen here with Dr Ralegh Radford, an authority on the period, examining a piece of pottery found on the site. (WMN)

This charming study of Churston Ferrers by W.J. Brunell dates from the mid-fifties. The village is recorded in Domesday. A seventeenth century manuscript says: 'Churchton or Churchston was originally held by the family of Bozun. William Bozun died about the beginning of Edward I's time, he left it to his daughters, one of whom, (Alice) married Sir Hugh Ferrers. It went through the Ferrers for many descents, finally to a daughter's family called Yard. In 1405 Joan Ferrers married Richard Yard of Bradley Manor and their descendents occupied Churston for 350 years'. The house 'Churston Court' is Elizabethan but was modernised in the 1850s and is now a hotel. The church (W.G. Hoskins, the historian, says that the dedication is unknown) has a plain west tower (on the right of the picture) of early date (about1300) but the remainder of the fabric is fifteenth century. (WMN)

Old cottages beside the road which leads from the main Brixham road to the church photographed in 1960. The bridge just visible in the background carried the Brixham Branch railway at the time. At this period there were twelve trains a day during the week and seventeen on Saturdays. The Brixham Branch was soon to be closed down; this came about in May 1963 and the lines were soon removed. (WMN)

Greenway is in the parish of Churston but one of its treasures is rarely seen. 'Greenway House' is a small Georgian mansion overlooking the River Dart. Sir Humphrey Gilbert was born in an earlier house in 1539. Newfoundland was discovered by John Cabot but in August 1583 it was Sir Humphrey who, in the name of Queen Elizabeth, formally took possession of the island. Richard Harvey was living at Greenway at the time the railway was being built; he refused to allow the railway company building the line to bridge the Dart to Dittisham, from whence it would have passed through the South Hams to Plymouth. Harvey's executors sold Greenway House to the Bolitho family who sold it to Sir Arthur Goodson in 1937. He in turn sold it to the Mallowans, Mrs Mallowan (better known as Agatha Christie) living there until her death. Her family still own it.

Thirteen
Stoke Gabriel

The road from Paignton to Stoke Gabriel is still narrow and winding. This has helped to keep the village isolated from the hustle and bustle of Torbay. Stoke has always included Sandridge and Waddeton. 'Sandridge House', a Grade II listed building, was built by Nash in 1805 and, after being in ruins for 30 years, was completely renovated recently. In 1991 it was for sale at an asking price of two million pounds. Also nearby is 'Waddeton House', an early nineteenth century house rebuilt in the Elizabethan style and adjacent to the ruins of an earlier house. It was owned for a short time by Mrs de Savary (wife of the yachtsman, and one-time owner of Lands End and other Cornish properties).

The inscription reads: 'Stoke Gabriel Church, engraved from Nature by W. Spreat'. This was published in 1842 when there were no other signs of human habitation visible. The parish church of St Mary and St Gabriel has a thirteenth century tower but the church itself is later, it was in a bad state of decay in the fifteenth century and had to be rebuilt. In the churchyard is an ancient yew tree, said to be between 1200 and 1500 years old, thus making it one of the oldest trees in England.

This photograph was taken well over a century later in 1970. The Misses Hamlin appended (unusually) a sad little note: 'The beauty of the scene makes it a favourite haunt for motorists, and for wealthy retired people who build new houses on the outskirts. In the last fifteen years the population has doubled and now stands at 1,300'.

The River Dart at Duncannon, Stoke Gabriel. The ferryman is attending to his boat on the left.

These were photographed by the staff of the now defunct *South Devon Journal* in 1958/57. Some of the charms of 'that bygone time' are still evident in the late 1990s.

Low tide on the Dittisham side of the River Dart at Stoke Gabriel.

The Church House Inn as seen from Church Walk with the lych-gate at the further end.

The Church House Inn, Stoke Gabriel's best-known hostelry. There is a local tradition that Stoke Gabriel once had a monastic house of some kind and that the inn is evidence of it. There is an account which reads: 'Some years ago the sexton was making excavations for a parish drain at the bottom of the orchard at the east end of the church and came across what was supposed to be the ruins of an old monastery'. The building may date from the fourteenth century when it would have housed the original builders of the church as well as being a refuge for fatigued travellers. It is still owned by the church authorities.

A snow plough in action in Stoke Gabriel, 2 January 1963. Perhaps a reminder that winters can be severe even in South Devon.

This records an interesting excavation undertaken by the Devon Archaeological (Exploration) Society under the eye of the late Ted Masson Phillips in 1958. The site was found at Lower Well Farm at Beastly Common, 'an isolated and wind-swept spot'. Coarse pottery (later identified as being Roman or Romano-British) and a spindle-whorl (used for spinning) were among the items recovered. Among food remains found were the shells of edible oysters. The comment was made: 'wherever the Romans were you always find oysters'. Its reason for existence remains uncertain and the ground 'reverted to its former privacy' at the end of the 'dig'.

A press photograph taken in Church Street showing a parade in costume celebrating the creation of the County Borough of Torbay, 1 April 1968. This lasted only six years as there was another reorganisation of local government in 1974. However, it is appropriate to end on an optimistic note. Torbay again achieves so-called 'unitary status' from 1 April 1998 and a new Town Council with full powers has been elected.

Acknowledgements

Torquay Museum has a wonderful pictorial archive of its own. Although primarily famous for its natural history collections (and its displays on the discoveries in Kents Cavern) the importance of collecting and maintaining illustrative records was realised long ago and there are now many thousands of pictorial and other images in its unique collections, put together because of the encouragement it gives to both its members and researchers from all over the world.

Two elderly ladies, the Misses Hamlin, were in charge of the Pictorial Records Section and they spent many hours mounting pictures, writing captions and sometimes travelling the district on bicycles for further pictures and information. They interested two local newspapers in the project, the *Western Morning News* and the *Torquay Times* (now defunct); their pictures from the 1950s and 1960s gave an added, contemporary dimension to the two ladies' work. These now have historic interest in their own right. The *Western Morning News* has kindly permitted its pictures to be reproduced here; each used has been indicated by the caption (WMN).

No volume on Paignton can be complete without giving its readers the opportunity to read further:

Brandon, Ruth. *Singer & the sewing machine*
Patterson, C.H. *History of Paignton 1953*
Penwill, F. Ralph. *Paignton in six reigns 1953*
Pike, J.R. Paignton. *Torbay's Heritage series 1993*
Tully, P. *Pictures of Paignton 1988*
Tully, P. *Pictures of Paignton, Part II 1992*
Tully, T. *Pictures of Paignton, Part III 1995*
Out of print items can be borrowed from local libraries.